Pocket Explorer

The Ancient Greek World

Richard Woff

INTERLINK BOOKS
An imprint of Interlink
Publishing Group, Inc.
www.interlinkbooks.com

In memory of John Sharwood Smith
τῷ κυρίῳ καὶ θρέψαντι

Author's acknowledgements
Thanks are due to the following colleagues for their advice and support: Sam Moorhead, Alexandra Villing, Lesley Kiely, Robert Knox, Paul Roberts and Jonathan Tubb.

First American edition published 2011 by
INTERLINK BOOKS
An imprint of Interlink Publishing Group, Inc.
46 Crosby Street, Northampton, Massachusetts 01060
www.interlinkbooks.com

Library of Congress Cataloging-in-Publication Data available.
ISBN: 978-1-56656-829-6

Designed by Crayon Design, Brighton
Printed in Singapore by Tien Wah Press

Illustration Acknowledgements

Main map artwork by Cally Sutherland, Crayon Design, Brighton.
Photographs are taken by the British Museum Department of Photography and Imaging, © The Trustees of the British Museum, unless otherwise stated below.

With kind permission of Jean-David Cahn and the Petrie Museum of Egyptian Archaeology: 10 top.
© Mark Daffey/Lonely Planet Images 24 bottom left.
Délégation Archéologique Française d'Afghanistan 29 bottom right.
Lesley Fitton 9 centre.
© Istockphoto/Viktor Prikhodko: 26 bottom.
Thomas Kiely 12 bottom left.
Robert Knox 29 centre
Sam Moorhead 4 bottom right, 6 top, 20 centre, 21 top, 22 top, 24 bottom right, 31 top.
© Österreichisches Archäologische Institut, photo N. Gail: 3, 16 bottom.
© Craig Perhouse/Lonely Planet Images 14 top.
Brian Stokes 4 top, 6 centre, 18 bottom left, 19 bottom left.
Jonathan Tubb 13 centre.
Richard Woff 8 centre, 9 top, 18 bottom right, 23 top, 31 bottom left.
Alexandra Villing 14 bottom left and right, 17 top left.

Contents

The Ancient Greeks

There is an ancient Greek story that Zeus, king of the gods, became so outraged by the bad behaviour of humans that he sent a huge flood to destroy them all; all, except a man called Deukalion and his wife Pyrrha. They survived the flood by building a wooden chest and hiding inside. Once the water had gone, they sowed stones in the earth from which arose a new generation of humans. The son of Deukalion and Pyrrha was Hellen – the ancient Greeks named themselves Hellenes after him, as do modern Greeks today.

The coast of the Peloponnese at the Mycenaean town of Asine.

View from the Cycladic island of Delos, birthplace of Apollo and Artemis.

Modern Greece consists of a mainland peninsula and a number of islands which spread across the eastern Mediterranean and along the coast of Turkey. Today, Greece is a single country with its capital at Athens on the mainland. In ancient times things were very different. Mainland Greece and the islands were divided into many small, independent regions called city-states because each was based around a town. But there were also Greek city-states all around the Mediterranean Sea and beyond as far as Russia and the borders of India. This book is not just about ancient Greece, but about the ancient Greek world – the places where Greeks lived and the different foreign peoples with whom they came into contact.

This figure is carved from the high-quality marble found on the Cycladic islands. It was made between 2600 and 2400 BC.

The ancient Greeks certainly saw themselves as Greeks and different from non-Greeks. Even though they were almost always at war with each other, they could still join together when threatened by foreigners, for example, the Persians in the fifth century BC. In spite of local differences, they shared religious beliefs, customs, styles of art and architecture, literature and language.

This man is speaking a line of poetry.

Language

The Greeks referred to non-Greek peoples as *barbaroi* – barbarians. This name came from the sound that foreign languages seemed to make to the Greeks: 'ba-ba'. The Greeks themselves did not all speak exactly the same language. Different groups of Greeks spoke different Greek dialects; for example, Athenians and people from Miletos spoke Ionic Greek, Spartans and Rhodians spoke Doric, Thebans and Lesbians spoke Aeolic. However, they were all able to understand each other.

Mythic travellers

The ancient Greeks were great travellers in real life and also in their myths. Odysseus was probably the most famous traveller as he wandered among strange peoples and monsters on his way home from the Trojan War. Jason too voyaged in his ship the *Argo* in search of the Golden Fleece. Herakles and Theseus both journeyed through Greece and beyond in search of adventures.

The sirens try to lure Odysseus and his crew on to the rocks.

Crete

The mountain range of Ida.

After he was born Zeus, king of the gods, was hidden by his mother in a cave on Mount Ida in Crete to protect him from his father. One of Zeus's sons was Minos, king of Crete and one of the judges of the dead. When, in the early twentieth century AD, the British archaeologist Sir Arthur Evans discovered the remains of a great prehistoric civilization on Crete, he named it the Minoan civilization after Minos.

The north entrance of the Minoan palace at Knossos.

Minoan civilization was based on a number of large palaces, the biggest being Knossos. The palaces were unusual because they did not have fortification walls. This suggests that the Minoans felt they had little to fear from outside invaders. The palaces were complicated, consisting of large numbers of rooms arranged around central courtyards. Some of the rooms were for official business, some were workshops, some places of worship, and many of them were store-rooms. Produce was probably brought in from the countryside around, stored and then handed out or traded from the palaces.

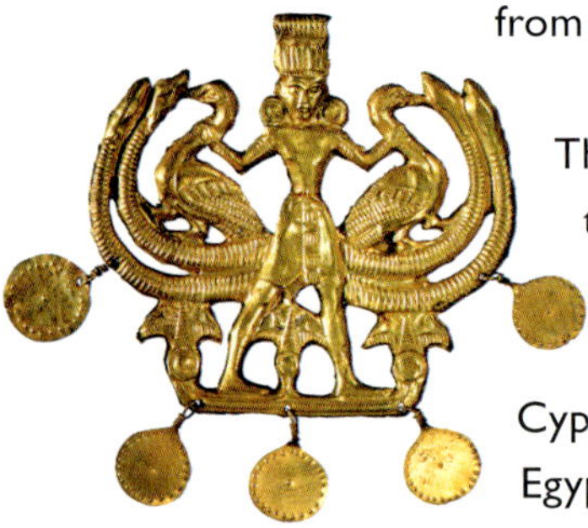

This gold pendant was influenced by Egyptian art, made by a Minoan craftsman and found on an island near Athens.

The Minoans were great seafarers and traded all over the eastern Mediterranean. Minoan towns and settlements have been found in Cyprus and elsewhere in the region. Egyptian wall paintings show Minoans bringing gifts to the pharaoh. Minoan-style wall paintings have been found in Israel and Egypt.

A lively octopus decorates this Minoan pot.

The importance of the sea is shown by the many Minoan pots which are decorated with sea creatures such as octopuses and dolphins.

A dangerous sport in Minoan Crete was bull-leaping.

Minoan artists were skilled at carving gemstones, metal-working, ivory-carving and pottery. Minoan palaces and houses were decorated with beautiful wall paintings on plaster. Many paintings and objects show bulls and bull horns. Bulls seem to have played an important part in Minoan religion and may have been symbols of the earthquakes that often hit the island. However, most experts agree that it was invaders from mainland Greece, and not earthquakes, that destroyed the Minoan palaces in about 1450 BC.

Theseus

Crete is best known for the story of Theseus and the Minotaur. Theseus was an Athenian prince who came to Crete and killed the bull-headed Minotaur, which lived in a maze called the labyrinth. The maze may reflect the complicated layout of Minoan palaces. Experts think that this myth may symbolize the defeat of the Minoans by invaders from mainland Greece.

Theseus and the Minotaur.

Writing

The Linear B writing on this clay tablet is a list of gifts of oil for gods and goddesses.

Linear B is the name given to a type of writing originally found on clay tablets at Knossos and then in mainland Greece. In the 1950s an architect named Michael Ventris was able to show that the language of Linear B was Greek. This helped archaeologists realise that the mainland Greeks had become rulers of Minoan Crete, not the other way round as Sir Arthur Evans had thought.

Mycenae and the Plain of Argos

Hundreds of Mycenaean figures like these were given as gifts to the gods

According to myth, the Trojan prince Paris and Helen, queen of Sparta, ran away together to Troy and sparked a war that lasted ten years. The Greek army that set off to get Helen back was led by Agamemnon, king of Mycenae. The fortress and palace of Mycenae lie on top of a hill that overlooks a large triangular plain. The plain was a source of plentiful crops, and pasture for cattle and horses, and had easy access to the sea.

The Lion Gate at Mycenae.

The walls of Mycenae are built from huge stones that were carefully shaped to fit together. The stones are so large that people used to believe that only giants could have been strong enough to build the walls. The way into the fortress and up towards the palace is through the Lion Gate. Two carved lions stand above the entrance – they may have been the symbol of the family that ruled here.

Mycenae has given its name to the period of Greek history from around 1600 to 1100 BC and the Greek people who lived in this period are called Mycenaeans even if they were not actually from Mycenae. Other Mycenaean sites in and around the plain include the city of Argos and Tiryns, another palace surrounded by mighty walls and the home of Herakles. There are also large fortresses, finely-built tombs, traces of roads and bridges and a huge dam.

Homer called Mycenae 'rich in gold'. This Mycenaean drinking cup may have been made by a Minoan craftsman.

View from the temple of Hera across the plain towards Argos.

In the seventh century BC a temple was built to the goddess Hera in the hills opposite Argos. Every year the people of Argos held a festival which linked the city and the surrounding countryside. They walked 10 km (6.2 miles) in a great procession across the plain from Argos to Hera's temple. The priestess of Hera rode in a cart pulled by oxen.

Troy

Mycenae and the city of Troy in northern Turkey were both explored in the nineteenth century by Heinrich Schliemann, a wealthy German archaeologist. Schliemann was convinced that there was some truth in the legend of the Trojan War. Troy was close to trade routes between the Mediterranean and the Black Sea and many modern archaeologists now agree that there may have been some conflict between the Greeks and the Trojans over trade.

Huge fortification walls at Troy (modern Hissarlik).

Rhodes

Mycenaean Greeks founded a trading settlement at Ialysos on the large island of Rhodes off the coast of Turkey. Archaeologists have discovered many rich Mycenaean graves there. Later, Rhodes became famous for a huge bronze statue of the sun god which stood at the mouth of the harbour. The statue, known as the Colossus of Rhodes, was one of the Seven Wonders of the World. It was toppled by an earthquake in 226 BC and may eventually have been melted down and turned into coins.

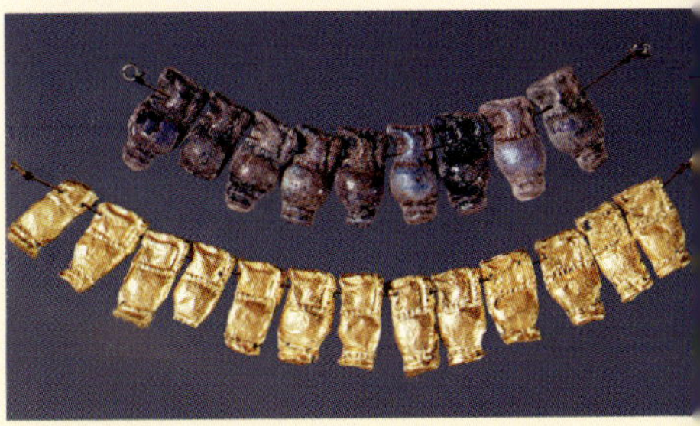

A necklace from the Mycenaean cemetery at Ialysos on Rhodes.

The Greeks in Africa

Throughout their history the ancient Greeks were aware of the powerful, wealthy and ancient kingdom of Egypt. Mycenaean Greeks appear in Egyptian wall paintings and luxury objects from, or influenced by, Egypt have been found in Mycenaean graves. Egypt was also a source of linen and papyrus. The annual flooding of the river Nile provided Egypt with rich land for growing wheat and other grain crops. These were important for the Greeks, whose land was less suited to producing grain. In return, the Egyptians imported wine, olive oil and silver from Greece.

This wine jar, made in an east Greek city, was found in Egypt. The Egyptian hieroglyphs on the neck are full of mistakes, so were probably written by a Greek.

Trade with Egypt was so important that in the seventh century BC, twelve Greek cities won permission from the Egyptian pharaoh Psammetikhos I to build a town in Egypt for their merchants. This was Naukratis, near the Mediterranean coast. The Greeks who lived and worked in Naukratis built temples and dedicated gifts to their own gods such as Apollo and Aphrodite. They imported Greek goods and exported Egyptian ones, but also manufactured pottery in Greek styles.

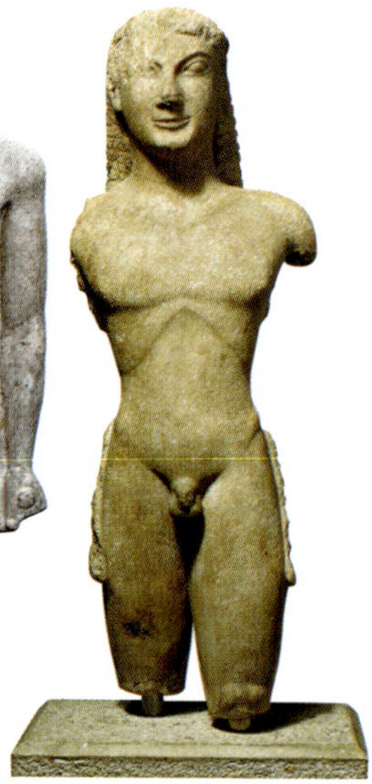

The Egyptian statue (left) and the Greek stand in the same pose.

Egyptian religious beliefs and artistic styles also spread around the Greek world. In Ionia, many Greeks started to bury their dead instead of cremating them. The idea of building large stone temples probably came from Egypt. The stone statues of men that the Greeks began to carve towards the end of the seventh century BC were influenced by Egyptian statues though their nudity is very typically Greek.

When Alexander the Great conquered Egypt, he founded the city of Alexandria. Alexandria became a famous centre of learning with a huge library and the first-ever museum. Near the entrance to the port of Alexandria stood the Pharos lighthouse, one of the Seven Wonders of the World. After Alexander, all the kings and queens of Egypt were Greek. The last of them was the famous Cleopatra. She was defeated in 31 BC by the Roman Octavian, who later became emperor Augustus. Egypt then became part of the Roman empire.

This coin of the Roman emperor Commodus shows the Pharos lighthouse.

Cyrene

Greeks from the island of Thera founded the city of Cyrene in north Africa (modern Libya) around 630 BC. The region around Cyrene was rich farmland and was especially famous for producing a plant called silphium, which was used as a medicine. There was also a freshwater spring at Cyrene that was sacred to the god Apollo.

The head of a bronze statue of a native north African inhabitant of Cyrene.

A silver coin of Cyrene showing a silphium plant.

The Ethiopians

The Greeks referred to black African peoples in general as 'Ethiopians'. They were aware of physical differences between peoples which they believed were due to the environment in which the people lived – Ethiopian comes from the Greek for 'burnt face'. The Greeks were certainly prejudiced against other peoples, though colour and physical appearance seem not to have been the most important reasons for this. According to Homer, the Ethiopians who lived south of Egypt were the favourites of the gods, who visited them regularly.

A small bronze jug with the girl's hair shown in great detail.

Cyprus and the Middle East

Copper was exported from Cyprus in blocks shaped like the skins of oxen.

Cyprus stands on several trade routes in the eastern Mediterranean. The island was rich in timber and in copper, which ancient peoples needed to make bronze. The Cypriots developed close links with the Mycenaean Greeks, from whom they adopted styles of pottery and metalwork, and with the Levant (modern Lebanon, Syria, Jordan, Israel and Palestine). The Greek language was introduced into Cyprus between 1250 and 1000 BC.

The wealth and position of Cyprus meant that neighbouring peoples wanted to capture and rule the island. In the eighth and seventh centuries BC, Cyprus was part of the Assyrian empire (based in modern Iraq) and in the sixth and fifth centuries, Egypt, Persia and Athens in turn struggled with each other to control the island. The Phoenicians from the coast of the Levant also had settlements in Cyprus and often came into conflict with the Greeks. The Phoenicians were probably the greatest seafarers in the ancient world and fought in the Persian navy at the battle of Salamis against the Greeks. They traded metals, luxury raw materials, textiles and other manufactured goods from the civilizations of the Levant and the Middle East.

Looking west from Kourion in the direction of Paphos, birthplace of Aphrodite.

Aphrodite, goddess of love, was born in Cyprus. She was sometimes called 'the Cyprian'.

A jug from Cyprus in the form of a bull.

About 125 km (77 miles) away to the east across the sea from Cyprus lay the port of Al Mina. Al Mina was set up as a trading post for Greek and Cypriot merchants around 800 BC and flourished for five hundred years. It was at the mouth of the river Orontes which provided an excellent trade route to the inland of what is now Syria. The Corinthians, who had strong connections with Al Mina, were the first Greeks to start to decorate their pottery and show human figures in ways borrowed from eastern civilizations. It was also from the east that the Greeks took some of their most famous mythical creatures, such as griffins and gorgons.

Griffins came to Greece from the Middle East. This Greek griffin was a decoration on a large bronze bowl.

This gold decoration shows eastern influence in the hairstyle of the centaur.

The Greek alphabet

Three rich Phoenician cities on the coast of modern Lebanon were Tyre, Sidon and Byblos. The Greeks named papyrus after Byblos and it is from that that the Greek word for book comes: *biblos*. Around 1000 BC the Greeks had lost the knowledge of writing, but some time in the early eighth century BC writing reappeared, using an alphabet borrowed from the Phoenicians. Different Greek regions used different versions of the alphabet, but eventually it was the Ionic version that became the one everyone used.

The Phoenician city of Byblos on the coast of modern Lebanon.

Phoenician		Greek	
𐤀	aleph	Α	alpha
𐤁	beth	Β	beta
𐤂	gimmel	Γ	gamma
𐤃	daleth	Δ	delta

The first four letters of the Phoenician and Greek alphabets.

Athens

In the fifth century BC Athens became the richest and most powerful of all the Greek city states. The city was near the sea so trade was easy. Athens had a good supply of silver from its mines and made high-quality pottery which was exported all round the Mediterranean, especially to the Etruscans in Italy. Between 490 and 479 BC the Athenians played a leading part in the defeat of Persian attempts to invade Greece. Once the Persians had been driven out of Greece, Athens created an alliance of Greek states to make sure that the Persians never again tried to conquer the Greeks. Over time, the threat from Persia faded away, but by then the Athenians had turned the alliance into an empire from which they gained vast amounts of money.

The Acropolis at Athens rises up in the centre of the city.

The Athenians used their wealth to build ships to strengthen their power at sea and to construct fine temples and other public buildings in Athens and in the surrounding countryside (called Attica). The finest temple of all was built on top of the hill called the Acropolis in the centre of Athens. This temple has become known as the Parthenon.

A washery for cleaning the silver mined at Laurion.

Cape Sounion at the southern tip of Attica. In myth, King Aigeus of Athens threw himself from these cliffs when he thought that his son Theseus had been killed by the Minotaur.

The Parthenon was built entirely out of marble from nearby Mount Pentelikon. Unlike most Greek temples, all the different parts of the Parthenon were decorated with marble sculptures painted in bright colours. Inside stood a 12-metre (39 feet) statue of Athena made of gold and ivory. All this was intended to show the connection between Athena and the city of Athens, and to demonstrate the bravery of Athenian citizens and the wealth and artistic talent of their city.

Two young Athenian horsemen from the frieze of the Parthenon.

By the end of the fifth century BC, only twenty years after the completion of the Parthenon, the Athenians had been defeated in a terrible war with the Spartans and their allies, supported by Persian money. However, Athens never really lost its influence. In the nineteenth century AD, when the Greeks had won their independence from Turkish rule, Athens became the national capital.

Silver and olives

This Athenian amphora (oil jar) shows men picking olives.

Olive oil was very important to life in Greece – it was used for cooking and eating, for lighting and also for cleaning the body. Attica produced very high-quality olive oil. It was given as a prize to winning athletes and was also exported widely. The tradition was that the olive tree had been given to Athens by the goddess Athena herself and you can see a sprig of olive on this Athenian coin (left). These coins were nicknamed 'owls' and were made from silver mined by slaves at Laurion on the east coast of Attica. The quality of the silver was so high that owls were used not only in Athens, but throughout the Mediterranean world.

The Greeks in the East

Pots decorated with wild goats were very popular in the Greek east in the 7th-6th centuries BC.

Good harbours, easily defended islands, closeness to other wealthy civilizations and to trade routes – all these reasons attracted Greek settlers to the coast of what is now Turkey. The Greeks who arrived here from the mid-eighth century BC onwards conquered or drove off local inhabitants or managed to live alongside them. Many of these Greek settlers came from the large island of Euboia and some perhaps from Athens. They became known as the Ionian Greeks.

Over time the Ionian cities grew in wealth and in the sixth century BC they were conquered by the Persians. Although Persian rule was quite fair, the Ionians became tired of paying taxes and of being required to provide soldiers and ships for their Persian rulers. In 499 BC, led by the city of Miletos, they revolted. With the help of Athens, they captured and burned Sardis, the local Persian capital. It took the Persian king Darius seven years to put down the revolt, but eventually he did so, sacking Miletos and either killing or enslaving its entire population. The help from Athens caused Darius to launch an attack on Greece that ended in his defeat at the battle of Marathon in 490 BC. Later in the fifth century BC, after the Greeks had defeated another Persian invasion, the Ionian Greeks gained their freedom from Persia, but became subjects of the Athenian empire.

The theatre at Ephesos could hold as many as 25,000 people.

Tombs at Xanthos in Lykia.

The great native kingdoms of the region, Lydia, Karia and Lykia, all developed close relationships with their Greek neighbours and with Greek culture. Lykian rulers built tombs above ground in their local tradition, but had them decorated with sculptures in the Greek style. Maussollos, ruler of Karia, had a huge tomb called the Mausoleum at Halikarnassos. It was decorated by the best Greek sculptors. Croesus, the fabulously wealthy king of Lydia, consulted the oracle at Delphi in mainland Greece and had superb gold gifts made for Apollo's temple there.

This statue from the Mausoleum is 3 m tall.

The Persian empire

The Persian king's palace at Persepolis was decorated with many fine carvings like this row of soldiers.

The Persians came originally from the south of the country that is now called Iran. Under their king, Cyrus the Great, they conquered an empire that stretched from the Mediterranean to India and from southern Russia to Egypt. The Persian empire was well-organized, with a good system of roads, local governors and several capital cities which the king visited in turn. The Greeks were suspicious of Persian power and wealth, but also impressed and intrigued.

In 401 BC a Persian prince named Cyrus tried to seize the throne from his older brother. In his army was a force of 10,000 Greek mercenary soldiers. When Cyrus was killed in battle, the 10,000 were stranded in enemy territory and had to march over 1,200 km from Babylon to reach the safety of the Greek cities near the Black Sea. Their adventures are described in a book by their general Xenophon.

Sparta, Corinth and Thebes

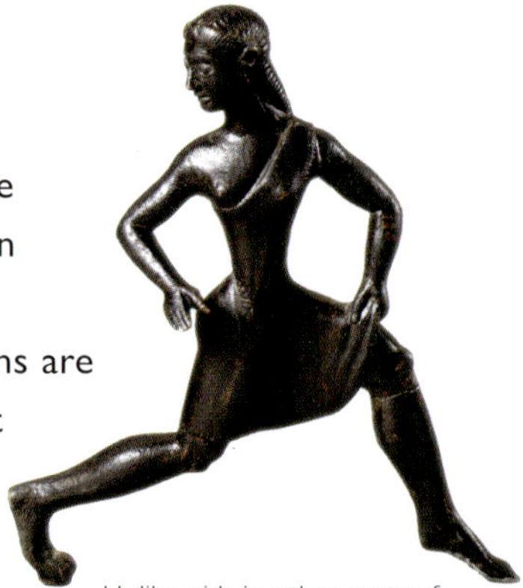

Unlike girls in other parts of Greece, Spartan girls were encouraged to exercise to keep fit.

The most southerly region of mainland Greece is called the Peloponnese and is joined to the rest of the mainland by an isthmus, or narrow strip of land. The Peloponnese is very mountainous and in winter the different regions are cut off from each other by snow. The largest fertile valley in the Peloponnese is the plain of Messenia. In the eighth century BC, the Spartans from a neighbouring valley conquered the Messenians and turned the whole population into their permanent slaves, called helots. In order always to be able to guard themselves against the helots, the Spartans developed a way of life that was designed to produce tough, ruthless fighters. Sparta was the most powerful city-state in the Peloponnese. The Spartans led the combined Greek army that finally drove the Persians out of Greece in 479 BC and later in the century won the long and costly Peloponnesian War against Athens.

A Spartan warrior.

View of the Taygetos mountains overlooking Sparta.

The roadway for dragging ships across the isthmus at Corinth.

The city of Corinth controlled the isthmus. A high hill called the Acrocorinth overlooks the site of the city which had plenty of fresh water from many springs in the area. These included Pirene, where in myth the hero Bellerophon captured the winged horse Pegasos. Corinth was a great trading city because of its easy access to the sea on both sides of the isthmus. Ships that wanted to travel from one side of Greece to the other were pulled up out of the water and dragged across on a stone roadway. This meant that they could avoid sailing round Cape Malea, the dangerous southern tip of the Peloponnese.

This tiny Corinthian jar contained perfume.

In the eighth and seventh centuries BC Corinthian pottery, decorated with exotic designs borrowed from the Middle East, was the most popular in the Greek world. By the sixth century BC, Athenian pottery had overtaken it. Over the years rivalry between Corinth and Athens caused many small conflicts, but finally was the spark that started the Peloponnesian War, in which Corinth fought on the Spartan side. Syracuse in Sicily, where the Athenians suffered a disastrous defeat, was a Corinthian colony.

In central Greece lay another of Athens' rival cities. Thebes lay on the plain of Boiotia, which was famous for horse-rearing. The city was said to have been founded by a Phoenician named Kadmos, who sowed in the earth the teeth of a dragon from which the first Thebans grew. Herakles and the god Dionysos were both said to be born in Thebes. Nearby was Mount Helikon, sacred to the Muses, who taught humans, poetry, music and other arts. The poets Hesiod and Pindar were both born in Boiotia. In the fourth century BC Thebes briefly became the strongest Greek city when it defeated Sparta, but in 335 BC, Alexander the Great destroyed it completely.

A Mycenaean tomb at Orchomenos near Thebes.

This terracotta figure is called a 'Tanagra' figurine, after the place in Boiotia where it was made.

The Greeks in the West

In the eighth century BC many Greeks settled in southern Italy and Sicily. They may have emigrated from their homelands because of overpopulation, famine or poverty. Or they may have moved to take advantage of the growth of trade offered by contact with foreign places. Most of the settlers came from mainland cities such as Corinth and Sparta and from the large island of Euboia. Local inhabitants were conquered by the Greeks or driven from their homes to live in neighbouring areas. The native people of Sicily remained fiercely resistant to the Greeks for many years.

The theatre was very popular among the Greeks of southern Italy. This pot shows a scene from a comedy.

The temple of Apollo at Paestum, south of the bay of Naples on the Italian coast.

The western Greek cities became important sources of grain for their mother cities and also traded with the rest of Greece. Several became fantastically wealthy and even sent out settlers of their own to other parts of the region. Some of the very best Greek temples are to be seen in Sicily and southern Italy.

The greatest of the western Greek cities was Syracuse in Sicily. It was founded by the Corinthians on a large natural harbour. In the early fifth century BC, Hieron was its ruler. He had fine temples built and brought to the city some of the greatest Greek writers. One of them, Pindar, wrote poems to celebrate the victories of Hieron and other rich Sicilians at the Olympic, Pythian and Isthmian Games.

This coin from Syracuse shows the nymph Arethousa, who tried to escape a Greek river god by diving into the sea.

In 415–13 BC, the Athenians attacked Syracuse in an attempt to prevent it supporting their enemies in the Peloponnesian War. The attack ended in a disastrous defeat and Athens went on to lose the war.

Stone quarries where the Syracusans imprisoned the defeated Athenians.

Under the rule of Dionysios I in the late fifth and early fourth centuries BC, Syracuse ruled most of Sicily. Dionysios defeated several attempts to conquer Sicily by Carthage, a powerful Phoenician city in north Africa. But Syracuse finally became part of the Roman empire when it was captured in 211 BC after a long siege. Archimedes, one of the greatest Greek scientists and mathematicians, died in this siege.

The Etruscans

Greek settlements in mainland Italy were mainly along the southern coast. The settlers soon came into contact with the Etruscans – a sophisticated and wealthy civilization further north. The Etruscans imported large numbers of Athenian pots to put in their tombs. Most of the Athenian pots in the British Museum come not directly from Greece, but from tombs in Etruria.

Etruscan artists often decorated objects with scenes from Greek myths as on this mirror showing Ajax, Thetis and Alcmene.

In search of tin

About 600 BC, Greeks from Phokaia in Ionia founded the city of Massilia (modern Marseilles) at the mouth of the river Rhône in southern France. To make bronze the Greeks needed tin, which was more plentiful in northern Europe than it was around the Mediterranean, and the Rhône provided an important trade route to the north. Greek objects have been found in burials near Paris and Munich and also in Switzerland. It was the Greeks who introduced the olive tree and the grapevine to France.

The Phokaians put a seal on their coins. *Phoce* means 'seal' in Greek.

All the Greeks Together

Every part of the Greek world had its own temples and sacred areas (called sanctuaries) where local people worshipped the gods. But there were also some sanctuaries which held festivals or ceremonies which were open to all Greeks wherever they lived.

The temple of Apollo at Delphi.

The Greeks believed that the centre of the world was at Delphi. High up in the mountains, it is perhaps the most beautiful place in Greece. Delphi was sacred to the god Apollo and people came there to consult the oracle, a priestess who could see the future. She was called the Pythia, after a snake called Python which Apollo killed at Delphi. All Greeks and also foreigners could consult the oracle. One of the most famous foreigners to come was Croesus, king of Lydia (now part of Turkey). He wanted advice about going to war against the Persians. The oracle told him that if he made war he would destroy a great empire. So he made war and did destroy an empire – his own!

Poseidon was god of horses as well as of the sea.

Chariot racing was so expensive that only rich people could afford to enter teams.

Sports competitions open to all Greeks were held at Delphi and also at Nemea and Isthmia – these are called panhellenic or 'all-Greek' games. The Nemean Games were in honour of Zeus, father of Herakles. Herakles had his first adventure at Nemea when he killed the Nemean Lion. The Isthmian Games, near Corinth, were in honour of

Poseidon. The most famous panhellenic games were of course at Olympia in honour of Zeus. In order to allow athletes to travel to Olympia safely, a holy truce was announced. This meant that fighting was supposed to stop for about a month before and after the festival. Athletes and spectators from all over the Greek world travelled to Olympia. Many of the most famous athletes were from cities outside mainland Greece, such as Syracuse, Tarentum and Gela.

The temple of Zeus at Nemea.

The panhellenic sanctuaries offered the Greek cities a good chance to compete against each other in other ways. The sanctuaries were full of buildings and statues that different cities set up in honour of the gods. Each of these was an attempt to outdo the other cities and to demonstrate their wealth or the artistic skill of their architects and sculptors. Often one city would set up a monument to thank the god for helping it to defeat another city.

Hieron I, ruler of the Greek city of Syracuse in Sicily, gave this Etruscan helmet as a gift to Zeus at Olympia to celebrate his victory over the Etruscans in 474 BC.

Eleusis

The sanctuary at Eleusis was sacred to the goddess Demeter and her daughter Persephone. Every year there was a festival called the Mysteries, at which people were introduced to secret rituals which gave them some hope for life after death. Eleusis was a district of Attica, but taking part in the Mysteries was open to anyone who spoke Greek.

This Athenian drinking cup shows Demeter (left) and Persephone with the hero Triptolemos who travelled in a winged chariot showing humans how to grow wheat.

Thessaly and Macedonia

The foreign witch Medea tricks the daughters of Pelias, a Thessalian king, into killing their father.

Thessaly, in the north of mainland Greece, contained two large plains, surrounded by mountains, which were rich in farmland and grazing. The Thessalians spoke a Greek dialect, but Thessaly was seen by the Greeks to the south as on the edge of the civilized world, a place of wildness and magic. The witches of Thessaly were said to be able to draw the moon down from the sky. Nevertheless, the Thessalians had some important cities and for a while were the leaders of the group of states that controlled the oracle of Delphi.

The mountain range that separates Thessaly from Macedonia to the north contains the highest mountain in Greece: Olympos, home of Zeus, the king of the gods. Not far away are the mountains of Pelion and Ossa, which the giants piled on top of each other in order to reach the top of Olympos during their battle with the gods. Macedonia had a huge central plain which was rich in cattle, sheep and horses as well as food crops. The region also supplied timber and metals such as silver, gold and iron.

Macedonia was occupied by the Persians for forty years until their withdrawal from Greece in 479 BC and the Macedonians fought for the Persians against the Greeks.

Olympos, the highest mountain in Greece and home of the Olympian gods.

In 1977 a tomb was discovered near the Macedonian capital of Aigai (modern Vergina). Its rich contents suggest that it was the tomb of King Philip II himself.

With Persian support, Alexander I became king of Macedonia in the early fifth century BC. Alexander claimed to be descended from Herakles, a claim that was kept alive a hundred years later by his descendant Philip II. Philip conquered neighbouring regions like Thessaly, and also brought all the city states of southern Greece under his rule. The southern Greeks deeply resented this, because they regarded the Macedonians as close to barbarians. However, Philip saw himself as a Greek and in 336 BC prepared to launch a war against Persia in revenge for their invasion of Greece. He was assassinated before he could go ahead, leaving his son Alexander II as king.

This bronze arrow-head has King Philip II's name on it.

This carving showing the fight between the centaurs and Thessalians comes from the temple of Apollo at Bassae in the Peloponnesian mountains.

Centaurs

Centaurs were mythical creatures – half horse and half man. They were wild and unpredictable and lived in mountain areas. A Thessalian king once invited the local centaurs to his wedding, but they got drunk and attempted to carry off the bride and the other women guests. The battle that followed was a favourite topic for Greek artists. An exception to the uncivilized character of centaurs was the wise centaur Kheiron. He was the teacher of several Greek heroes including Achilles, the best of the Greek warriors who fought at Troy. Achilles' home was Phthia in Thessaly.

Cavalry

Unlike the rest of Greece, Thessaly and Macedonia had large open plains that were suitable for rearing horses. The Thessalians were the best cavalry in Greece. In the Macedonian armies of Philip and Alexander, the Thessalian cavalry became a very powerful and important fighting force.

A galloping horse on a coin from the city of Larissa in Thrace (left) and a cavalryman on a Macedonian coin of Alexander the Great.

The Greeks in the North

Wheat was very important in the ancient Greek diet. This woman is grinding wheat to make bread or porridge.

Thrace, to the north-east of mainland Greece, was not Greek-speaking. This meant that the Greeks had no hesitation about using Thracians as slaves. The Thracians fiercely resisted the settlements that the Greeks established along the coast of their region, but were not organized enough to be able to drive them away. In spite of their resistance to the Greeks, Thracian leaders were keen to possess fine Greek luxury goods, many of which have been found in their tombs. Thrace was an important source of food crops such as wheat, and gold and silver were also mined in the region. Another Greek city in Thrace, Byzantium, was to become the most important city in the Greek world in the fourth century AD.

Orpheus playing the lyre with two warriors dressed in Thracian cloaks and hats.

Like Thrace, the area round the Black Sea supplied the Greek world with grain and gold. Greek settlers, mainly from Miletos in Ionia, founded cities along the coasts. Local inhabitants were suspicious of these foreigners, but also keen to benefit from the opportunities for trade that they offered. The Scythians, who lived in what is now southern Russia, were a nomadic people. They traded raw gold from central Asia with the Greek cities on the coast. A Scythian grave near Olbia contained Scythian weapons and armour, an Athenian wine cup and two jars of wine from the Greek island of Chios.

Khersonesos: a Greek city on the coast of the Black Sea in southern Russia.

This gold clothing decoration shows two Scythian archers back to back.

As riders, Scythians preferred trousers to Greek tunics and robes. To the Greeks, trousers were an unmistakeable sign of being a barbarian. Nevertheless, Athens had 300 government-owned Scythian slaves whose job it was to act as a police force and keep order around the marketplace and law courts of the city.

A bronze coin from Olbia shaped like a dolphin.

Athens and Thrace

The thick forests of Thrace were an important source of the timber that Athens needed for shipbuilding. Thracian mercenary soldiers fought for Athens during its war with Sparta. The Athenians also adopted a Thracian goddess named Bendis and every year held a procession in her honour in which both Athenians and native Thracians took part.

A carved slab showing a group of worshippers approaching the goddess Bendis.

Amazons

Other mythical inhabitants of this region were the Amazons – a tribe of women who lived without men, rode horses and were fierce warriors. This was the complete opposite of how women were supposed to behave in Greek culture and the Greeks saw it as another example of wild, uncivilized, un-Greek behaviour. In Greek stories, whenever the Amazons fight Greek male heroes such as Herakles, Achilles or Theseus, the Amazons always lose!

This bronze figure shows how skilful Amazons were at riding and at shooting the bow.

Alexander the Great and his Empire

This marble head of Alexander may be from Alexandria in Egypt.

Philip II of Macedonia was murdered and his son Alexander became king. Alexander completed the conquest of Greece by defeating an uprising of Greek cities led by Athens. In 334 BC, Alexander began the war against the Persians that his father had been preparing for when he died. In just ten years, he conquered the whole of the Persian empire which stretched from Turkey to Iraq and from Egypt to the borders of India. Although many Greeks did not consider Macedonians to be really Greek, it was Alexander who set the scene for Greek language and culture to spread further than it ever had before.

Alexander was only 33 when he died in Babylon in 323 BC. His huge empire was divided up among his generals. Ptolemy became the first Greek king and pharaoh of Egypt; Ptolemy's descendant Cleopatra was the last of his family to rule before she was defeated by the Romans and committed suicide. Seleukos became ruler of Asia. It was the royal families of these generals who over the years brought Greek culture to their regions. While local customs and languages continued to exist, the rulers built temples, theatres and sometimes whole cities in the Greek style. They invited visits from Greek writers and thinkers and they made Greek the official language.

This inscription (carved writing) is from Priene, a Greek city in Ionia, where Alexander helped pay for a temple to Athena. The first line reads: BASILEUSALEXANDROS (King Alexander).

This coin from the Greek kingdom of Bactria in Afghanistan has an Indian goddess and writing on one side and Greek on the other.

Alexander the God

In the western desert of Egypt, at the oasis of Siwa, lay the temple of Zeus Ammon. Ammon was the Greek name for Amun, greatest of the Egyptian gods, so Zeus Ammon was a combination of the two chief gods of Greece and Egypt. Like his father, Alexander claimed that he was descended from Herakles, son of Zeus. This coin shows Alexander wearing the horns of Zeus Ammon as the son of the god.

There is an ancient Greek city called Ai Khanoum. It was founded in about 330 BC and destroyed in about 130 BC. The city has some typical Greek buildings: a gymnasium where people could train and exercise as athletes and a theatre for the performance of plays. It also has a palace and two temples built in a Persian style. Inside one of the temples stood a huge statue, perhaps of Zeus. It was made mainly of wood with some parts in stone, including a beautifully carved marble foot wearing a perfect Greek sandal. When we think about the ancient Greek world, it is worth remembering not just the Acropolis at Athens, but also this Greek statue of the Greek king of the gods standing in a Persian-style temple in a city far away in northern Afghanistan.

The valley of the river Swat in Pakistan where Alexander the Great fought two battles against the local inhabitants.

A sculpture from Gandhara (modern Pakistan) showing the Trojan horse.

The marble foot from a temple in Ai Khanoum.

From Then to Now

A painting of John the Baptist from Constantinople; about AD 1300.

The first parts of the Greek world to come under the control of Rome were the cities of south Italy and Sicily. Greece itself was conquered in 146 BC when Corinth was destroyed. The art, literature and culture of Greece had a huge influence on the Romans – the Roman poet Horace even commented that 'conquered Greece conquered its conqueror'. In AD 324 the Roman emperor Constantine made the Greek city of Byzantium the new capital of the empire and renamed it Constantinople. By this time, Greek had become the official language of Christianity and Constantinople became a great centre of learning. Rome and the western empire fell to barbarian invaders in the fifth century AD, but over the next 500 years the Greek Byzantine empire based on Constantinople increased in power and size.

This picture shows the explosion which damaged the Parthenon in Athens in AD 1687. The temple had been turned into a mosque. You can see its minaret.

From the eleventh century AD, the Byzantine empire slowly weakened under pressure from powers such as the Ottoman Turks. When the Turks captured Constantinople in 1453, scholars from the university there fled west to Rome, bringing with them copies of some of the great works of ancient Greek literature. Muslim scholars translated ancient Greek works into Arabic so they could use them in their own studies. Greece remained under Turkish rule for more than 300 years. The Parthenon, which

Christians had made into a church, was now turned into a mosque, but the Greeks were not forced to give up their Christian religion.

Byzantium was renamed Constantinople and is now known as Istanbul. The name Istanbul may come from the Greek meaning 'to the city'.

In the eighteenth century, as western European powers such as Britain, France and Russia started to compete for control of the eastern Mediterranean, the Ottoman empire grew weaker. At the same time, more western scholars and artists were travelling to Greece, drawn there by their interest in ancient Greek culture. After a long war, the Greeks won their independence from Turkish rule in 1832. The first king of the independent Greece was Othon, a German prince, who ruled for 30 years. He made Athens the capital and had all the later buildings cleared from the Acropolis leaving just the Parthenon and the other ancient buildings as symbols of the new country. By the 1920s, Macedonia, Crete, Thessaly, part of Thrace and some of the islands near Turkey had been added to the country.

A Greek Cypriot shop in north London.

In the twentieth century Greece experienced unsettled times with periods of civil war, interference by foreign powers, rule by the military and tension with neighbouring Turkey. In 1981 a fully democratic Greece joined the European Union. In 2004 Athens hosted the Olympic Games, when the festival returned to its homeland for the first time since the first modern games in 1896. Even though there is now one united Greece, Greeks continue to live in and enrich many different parts of the world from Britain to South Africa and from the USA to Australia.

A modern Greek euro shows its ancient origins (see page 15).

Further Reading

The Ancient Greek Olympics, Richard Woff,
British Museum Press, 1999

The British Museum Illustrated Encyclopaedia of Ancient Greece, Sean Sheehan, British Museum Press, 2002

Fun Book: Ancient Greece, Sandy Ransford,
British Museum Press, 1999

Island of the Minotaur: The Greek Myths of Ancient Crete,
Sheldon Oberman (text) & Blair Drawson (illustration),
Crocodile Books/Interlink, 2005

Pocket Timeline: Ancient Greece, Emma McAllister,
British Museum Press, 2006

For older readers:

A Traveller's History of Greece,
Tim Boatswain & Colin Nicolson,
Interlink Publishing, 2007

A Traveller's History of Athens, Richard Stoneman,
Interlink Publishing, 2004

Ancient Greece: An Explorer's Guide,
Robert Emmet Meagher & Elizabeth Parker Neave,
Interlink Publishing, 2008

Athens: A Cultural and Literary History, Michael Llewellyn Smith,
Interlink Publishing, 2004

Art for Travellers Greece, Bill and Lorna Hannan,
Interlink Publishing, 2006

You can find additional information by visiting the Interlink website:
www.interlinkbooks.com